YOGA FOR EVERYONE

YOGA ON YOUR BACK AND BELLY

BY LAURA VILLANO, RYT
ILLUSTRATED BY CHRISTOS SKALTSAS

BLUE OWL
BOOKS

TIPS FOR CAREGIVERS

The practice of yoga helps us learn about our breath and body, how the two are connected, and how they can help us acknowledge our feelings without letting them overwhelm us. This awareness can help us navigate different situations at school or at home. Yoga gives us tools to be the best versions of ourselves in every situation. Plus, moving our bodies feels good!

SOCIAL AND EMOTIONAL GOALS

After reading this book, kids will be able to use their yoga practice to:

1. Become more aware of their emotions and the physical sensations they produce in the body (self-awareness).

2. Use the techniques included in the text to help manage their emotions and de-stress (self-management).

TIPS FOR PRACTICE

Encourage self-awareness and self-management with these prompts:

Before reading: Ask students to check in with themselves. How do they feel, in both mind and body?
Emotional example: What kinds of thoughts are you having?
Physical example: How does your body feel today?

During reading: Encourage students to check in as they move through the book.
Emotional example: How does it feel when you close your eyes and focus on your breathing?
Physical example: How do certain poses feel in your body?

After reading: Take time to reflect after practicing the poses.
Emotional example: How do you feel after practicing yoga?
Physical example: Are there certain poses you like or don't like?

TABLE OF CONTENTS

BEFORE YOU BEGIN YOUR PRACTICE, YOU WILL NEED:

- Yoga mat (A towel or blanket works, too!)
- A prop (wooden blocks or books work well)
- Comfy clothes so you can move around easily
- Water to stay hydrated
- A good attitude and an open mind!

By practicing the poses in this book, you understand any physical activity has some risk of injury.
If you experience pain or discomfort, please listen to your body, discontinue activity, and ask for help.

CHAPTER 1

NAMASTE!

Namaste (nah-mah-stay)! This is how we greet each other when we practice **yoga**. We place our palms together in front of our chests when we say it. We slightly bow our heads. In this book, you will learn some back and belly **poses**!

Begin seated on your mat. You can cross your legs. Or sit on your heels with your legs under you. **Focus** on keeping your back straight. Draw your shoulders down your back. Keep your arms by your sides or rest them in your lap.

CHAPTER 2

LET'S PRACTICE!

❯ Put your hand on your stomach.

❯ **Inhale** through your nose. Feel the air fill up your belly.

❯ **Exhale**. Feel your belly relax as the air leaves your nose.

❯ Repeat this 10 times.

Let's start with belly poses!

CHILD'S POSE PART 1

❯ Begin in a table position. Your hands and knees should both be on the mat.

CHILD'S POSE PART 2

> Bring your big toes together. Keep your knees wide.

> Shift your hips back toward your heels.

> Reach your arms out in front of you.

> Rest your forehead on the mat.

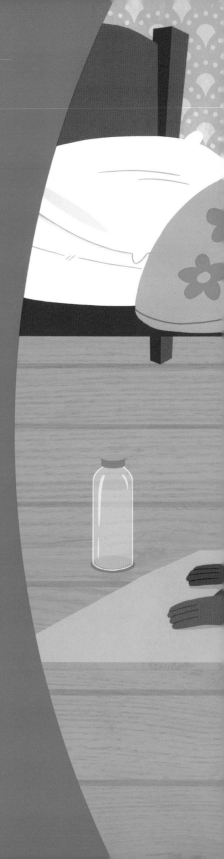

TIP: Try walking your hands to the right. Do you feel a stretch on your left side? Try the other side!

COBRA POSE

❯ Make your way onto your belly. Your legs should be stretched out behind you.

❯ Lift up onto your elbows, keeping your forearms and hands on the mat.

❯ Keep your elbows close to your body.

❯ As you inhale, lift your head and chest off of the mat. This is Cobra Pose.

DID YOU KNOW?

A lot of yoga poses are named after the animals they look like. Can you see how you look like a snake in this pose?

TIP: Keep your shoulders relaxed and away from your ears!

BOW POSE

❯ Rest back down on your belly.

❯ Place your forehead on the mat.

❯ Bend both of your knees. Your feet should go toward the back of your head.

❯ Reach your arms behind you and grab your ankles.

❯ Inhale. As you exhale, reach your feet toward the ceiling and your thighs away from the floor. This will help lift your **torso** off the mat.

Bow Pose stretches your back. Can you feel it?

TIP: Some poses are tough! Take your time and breathe. Focus on moving slowly with your breath.

BRIDGE POSE

Are you ready to try poses on your back? Let's start with Bridge Pose.

❯ Lie on your back with your arms long by your sides.

❯ Keep your palms flat on the mat.

❯ Bend your knees so your feet are planted firmly on the mat.

❯ Keep your feet about hip width distance apart.

❯ Lift your hips up off of the mat. Reach them toward the ceiling.

TIP: Focus on staying strong in your legs and torso!

HAPPY BABY POSE

❯ Rest your hips back on the floor.

❯ Bend your knees up toward your armpits. The bottoms of your feet should face up toward the ceiling.

❯ Grab your feet.

❯ Rock side to side.

Play around in this pose! Can you see why it is called Happy Baby?

TIP: Try to straighten one leg at a time. How does this feel?

RECLINED TWIST

❱ Lie flat on your back.

❱ Reach your arms up overhead to give yourself a full body stretch.

❱ Bring your right knee toward your chest.

❱ Use your left hand to guide your right knee across your body.

❱ Rest your knee on a yoga block or on the floor.

❱ Stretch your right arm out straight to your side. Look over your right shoulder.

❱ Rest in this twist for 10 breaths.

❱ Now try the other side!

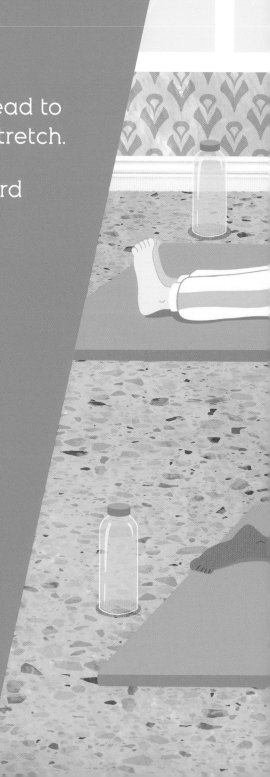

CHAPTER 3

REFLECT

Nice job! Now, lie flat on your back and relax your muscles. If it feels comfortable, close your eyes. Inhale and exhale 5 times. Take some time to **reflect**. How does your body feel?

Are you ready to practice again tomorrow? Show the new poses you learned to a friend!

GOALS AND TOOLS

GROW WITH GOALS

Set a goal to practice yoga every day!
Here are some ideas to get you started.

1. See how it feels to start your day with a yoga pose! Before you get out of bed in the morning, practice your Reclined Twist. Try this for a week.

2. Before you go to bed at night, practice Child's Pose. Try this for a week. See how it feels to bring yoga into your routine every night.

TRY THIS!

You can use a prop for support as you practice Bridge Pose.

1. Lie on your back with your arms long by your sides and palms facedown.

2. Bend your knees so your feet are planted firmly on the mat.

3. Lift your hips up off of the mat. Reach them toward the ceiling.

4. Place a prop under your hips and rest here for some time.

REFLECT: See how this changes the pose. What feels different from the more active pose you did earlier?

GLOSSARY

exhale
To breathe out.

focus
To concentrate on something.

inhale
To breathe in.

namaste
A common greeting in yoga. It means, "The spirit in me honors and acknowledges the spirit in you."

poses
Positions or postures.

reflect
To think carefully or seriously about something.

torso
The part of your body between your neck and your waist, not including your arms.

yoga
A system of exercises and meditation that helps people control their minds and bodies and become physically fit.

TO LEARN MORE

Finding more information is as easy as 1, 2, 3.

1. Go to www.factsurfer.com
2. Enter "**yogaonyourbackandbelly**" into the search box.
3. Choose your cover to see a list of websites.

INDEX

Blue Owl Books are published by Jump!, 5357 Penn Avenue South, Minneapolis, MN 55419, www.jumplibrary.com

Copyright © 2020 Jump! International copyright reserved in all countries. No part of this book may be reproduced in any form without written permission from the publisher.

Library of Congress Cataloging-in-Publication Data

Names: Villano, Laura, author.
Title: Yoga on your back and belly / by Laura Villano.
Description: Blue owl books. | Minneapolis, MN: Jump!, Inc., [2020]
Series: Yoga for everyone
Includes index.
Audience: Ages 7–10 | Audience: Grades 2–3
Identifiers: LCCN 2019031140 (print)
LCCN 2019031141 (ebook)
ISBN 9781645271932 (hardcover)
ISBN 9781645271949 (paperback)
ISBN 9781645271956 (ebook)
Subjects: LCSH: Hatha yoga—Juvenile literature.
Classification: LCC RA781.7 .V54 2020 (print)
LCC RA781.7 (ebook)
DDC 613.7/046—dc23
LC record available at https://lccn.loc.gov/2019031140
LC ebook record available at https://lccn.loc.gov/2019031141

Editor: Jenna Trnka
Designer: Anna Peterson
Illustrator: Christos Skaltsas

Printed in the United States of America at Corporate Graphics in North Mankato, Minnesota.